W9-BGS-127

BACKYARD ANIMALS
HUMMINGBIRDS

by Kristin Petrie

Checkerboard
Library

An Imprint of Abdo Publishing
www.abdopublishing.com

www.abdopublishing.com

Published by Abdo Publishing, a division of ABDO, PO Box 398166, Minneapolis, Minnesota 55439.
Copyright © 2015 by Abdo Consulting Group, Inc. International copyrights reserved in all countries. No part of this book may be reproduced in any form without written permission from the publisher. Checkerboard Library™ is a trademark and logo of Abdo Publishing.

Printed in the United States of America, North Mankato, Minnesota.
102014
012015

THIS BOOK CONTAINS
RECYCLED MATERIALS

Cover Photos: Alamy, iStockphoto
Interior Photos: Alamy pp. 5, 8, 10, 19, 28; Corbis p. 25; Glow Images pp. 1, 21, 23, 29; iStockphoto pp. 6, 15, 16, 17; MICHAEL & PATRICIA FOGDEN/MINDEN PICTURES/National Geographic Creative pp. 9, 27; Science Source pp. 13, 14, 20

Series Coordinator: Megan M. Gunderson
Editors: Tamara L. Britton, Bridget O'Brien
Art Direction: Neil Klinepier

Library of Congress Cataloging-in-Publication Data

Petrie, Kristin, 1970- author.
  Hummingbirds / Kristin Petrie.
     pages cm. -- (Backyard animals)
  Audience: Ages 8-12.
  Includes index.
  ISBN 978-1-62403-661-3
1. Hummingbirds--Juvenile literature. I. Title.
  QL696.A558P48 2015
  598.7'64--dc23
                              2014024662

TABLE OF CONTENTS

Hummingbirds. 4

Origin & Range 6

Habitat 8

Flying Jewels 12

Nests & Babies 16

Nectar & Bugs 18

Behavior 22

Communication 24

Enemies & Defenses 26

Conservation 28

Glossary. 30

Websites 31

Index .32

HUMMINGBIRDS

What flying creature hovers on invisible wings? This bird flaps its wings up to 70 times every second. It can even fly backward! What is this creature? It is the colorful hummingbird.

Hummingbirds belong to the scientific order Apodiformes. The hummingbird family, Trochilidae, has two subfamilies. One is the hermit hummingbird family, Phaethornithinae. The other is the typical hummingbird family, Trochilinae.

Currently there are more than 100 hummingbird **genera**. Within those groups, there are more than 300 species! Just over 30 of these are hermit hummingbirds. The rest are typical hummingbirds.

Some hummingbirds are found in North America. Do you live in the Midwest or on the East Coast? Ruby-throated hummingbirds might pass through your area. In the Southwest, calliope, Costa's, and other hummingbirds are common. Allen's, Anna's, and rufous hummingbirds are two of the species found in the West.

SCIENTIFIC CLASSIFICATION

Kingdom: Animalia
Phylum: Chordata
Class: Aves
Order: Apodiformes
Family: Trochilidae

A male calliope hummingbird
has bright feathers at its throat.

ORIGIN & RANGE

Little is known about the hummingbird's history. Hummingbird bones are **porous**. Some are even hollow! So, tiny hummingbird fossils are rare. Still, **ornithologists** believe these small birds **evolved** from other birds about 40 million years ago. Some scientists believe hummingbirds are originally from Europe or Asia, but they are no longer found there. Now, they only live in the **New World**.

Today, the hummingbird's range is large. The tiny, warm-blooded birds are found throughout the Western **Hemisphere**. Most of these **tropics**-loving birds live in South America. More than half of all species live in the South American countries of Ecuador and Brazil.

Around 12 species venture north to the United States and Canada. Some species travel as far north as Alaska! For example, the rufous hummingbird spends summer months in southern Alaska. It **migrates** all the way back to Mexico for winter.

The rufous hummingbird migrates farther than any other hummingbird in North America.

North America

Central America

South America

Where Hummingbirds Live

N

North America

South America

Europe

Asia

Africa

Australia

HABITAT

The red-billed streamertail is native to Jamaica.

Even though they prefer warm climates, hummingbirds live in a variety of **habitats**. **Lush** places such as rain forests top the list. However, hummingbirds also live in deserts, coastal lowlands, high mountain ranges, and pine forests.

For example, the Costa's hummingbird occupies desert regions in Southern California and Mexico. Other species thrive in the Andes Mountains at 16,000 feet (4,800 m) above **sea level**. Some hummingbirds live only on islands in the Caribbean Sea.

Hummingbirds can survive in human-made **environments** as well. They live on agricultural land, such as banana and coffee plantations. They also make their homes in large cities, small towns, and even backyards. Any place with brightly colored flowers or bird feeders meets the little flier's greatest need, which is food.

The violet-tailed sylph lives in Ecuador and Colombia.

Hummingbirds such as this ruby-throated
hummingbird may return to the same
summer or winter perch in different years.

Some hummingbirds **migrate** to new **habitats** as the seasons change. They prepare for migration by eating as much as they can. This increases their weight by up to 50 percent. The extra food converts to fat, which provides energy for their long, challenging flights.

Each hummingbird species has its own migration plan. The birds fly alone. Some hummingbirds travel more than 3,000 miles (4,800 km)! The ruby-throated hummingbird flies 500 miles (800 km) across the Gulf of Mexico without stopping. Other hummingbirds that cross water may rest on ships before continuing their journeys.

Northward migration begins as early as February and continues during the spring. Hummingbirds head back south in August and September. Some hummingbirds don't migrate long distances. Instead, they simply move up or down in elevation depending on seasonal temperature changes.

Male hummingbirds generally migrate first. Females and young hummingbirds follow later. This staggered migration protects the hummingbird's population. There wouldn't be enough food if every bird traveled together all at once.

NO HITCHHIKING!
People used to think hummingbirds traveled on the backs of larger birds!

FLYING JEWELS

Everyone knows one thing about hummingbirds. They are small! The average hummingbird weighs 0.1 to 0.2 ounces (3 to 6 g). Bee hummingbirds average just 0.07 ounces (2 g). They weigh less than a penny! The giant hummingbird species weighs ten times that, at 0.7 ounces (20 g). Yet that's not so giant. A common crow weighs a full 16 ounces (450 g).

On average, hummingbirds measure 2.4 to 4.7 inches (6 to 12 cm) long. The bee hummingbird measures just 2.2 inches (5.5 cm). The giant hummingbird reaches 7.9 inches (20 cm) long. Some female hummingbirds are larger than males.

The hummingbird's delicate body has a small head with a long bill and dark eyes. The eyes are high on the head so the hummingbird can see enemies above. The birds can even see **ultraviolet** light. This allows for spotting bright flowers and distinguishing between species. On the other hand, hummingbirds have a poor sense of smell.

Hummingbirds have thick necks, broad chests, thin legs, and tiny feet. There are four toes on each foot. Three face forward and one faces backward. Some birds have short toenails while others have long, sharp claws.

The bee hummingbird is the smallest bird in the world. It is found in Cuba and on several other nearby islands.

The small feet are very weak and cannot hold the bird's weight for walking. They are only useful for perching. Hummingbirds must fly from perch to perch to move about. Strong, highly adapted wings meet this need.

TINY FEET

The order Apodiformes means "unfooted birds." The hummingbird doesn't wander around on the ground like a crow or a robin might do. It only uses its feet for perching.

Female (*left*) and male (*right*) ruby-throated hummingbirds have very different coloring.

The hummingbird's wings have specialized bones and muscles. The muscles used for flight make up one-fourth of the hummingbird's weight. And, hummingbirds can rotate their wings 180 degrees. This allows movement forward, backward, sideways, up and down, and even upside down! Hummingbirds fly up to 30 miles per hour (45 km/h).

Hummingbirds are known for their vibrant colors. The most colorful hummingbirds are generally male. Deep metallic red, orange, green, and blue **iridescent** feathers may mark the male's head, back, belly, crest, tail, or **gorget**.

Females, babies, and hermit hummingbirds are less colorful. They are generally brown, reddish, or gray in color. Their drab coats attract less attention. This helps them avoid predators and draw less attention to nests.

THE HUMMINGBIRD

EYE

BILL

WING

FEET

TAIL

NESTS & BABIES

Hummingbirds may build nests in the same place for several years in a row. Some nests are close to the ground. Others are 100 feet (30 m) up!

Female hummingbirds build nests after mating. Mating happens in spring and summer, when food is plentiful. Male hummingbirds attract females with their vibrant colors, daring flight displays, and melodic songs.

The female hummingbird spends 1 to 14 days creating the perfect nest. It may be built in a tree, on a ledge, or even on a cactus. Feathers, fur, and other materials make the inside soft. The outside is made with bark, moss, leaves, and lichen to help the nest blend in with its surroundings. The nest is held together with spider webs.

When the nest is complete, the mother hummingbird lays her first egg. She lays a second egg approximately 48 hours later. The eggs are tiny, white ovals. They measure just 0.3 to 0.8 inches (0.8 to 2.0 cm) and are the smallest of any bird. The mother

incubates the eggs for 16 to 19 days. Some eggs hatch at the same time. Others hatch as they were laid, hours apart.

Hummingbirds are born blind, naked, and helpless. Their mother keeps their tiny, warm-blooded bodies safe using her own body. This is called brooding. It lasts for 6 to 18 days.

Nestlings leave the nest around one month after birth. Now called **fledglings**, they continue returning to the nest for protection and feeding for another three to four weeks. Those making it to adulthood live 6 to 12 years.

As hummingbirds grow, they stretch out their nest.

NECTAR & BUGS

What do hummingbirds eat? Nectar, of course! Approximately 90 percent of their diet is from nectar. This sugary liquid is produced by flowers. Hummingbirds visit up to 1,000 flowers each day! They **pollinate** each flower as they feed. Hummingbirds also love to eat from backyard feeders.

Hummingbirds have good memories. Individuals remember the flowers in their territory and how long they take to refill with nectar. Hummingbirds also remember where feeders are, even along **migration** routes.

The other 10 percent of the hummingbird's diet comes from insects, including ants, beetles, flies, spiders, and wasps. Hummingbirds use their impressive flying skills to pursue insects. They will catch insects in midair and pluck them from plants. They even steal insects from spider webs!

Contrary to popular belief, the hummingbird's bill is not a straw. The hummingbird has a split bill like other birds. It opens its bill to let out its long, extendable tongue. The hummingbird laps nectar onto its tongue 13 times per second. It closes its bill to swallow.

A young ruby-throated hummingbird showing off its bill

A BIG CROWD

A group of hummingbirds is called a charm of hummingbirds.

When possible, hummingbirds will perch to feed because it saves energy.

Hovering is the reason hummingbirds can get to the nectar they want. But, not all hummingbirds are able to feed on all flowers. Bill shape and size differ between species and the type of flowers in their **habitat**. Certain bills fit perfectly into certain flowers. This allows different hummingbird species to feed in the same region without wiping out the supply of nectar.

Hummingbird bills are generally long and slender, but some have special features. The sword-billed hummingbird's bill is four inches (10 cm) long. That is longer than its body! The thornbill has a relatively short bill. The lucifer hummingbird's bill curves downward. But the awlbill and avocetbill have bills that curve up.

Racing from flower to flower and hovering to feed is hard work. So, hummingbirds eat about half their weight in sugar every day. They feed five to eight times an hour. Mother hummingbirds feed their young twice an hour by **regurgitating** what they've eaten. Hummingbirds also need to drink water. Some water comes from nectar. The rest comes from drinking from wet leaves.

A sword-billed hummingbird can share a feeder with speckled hummingbirds. But, it can reach different types of flowers with its long bill.

BEHAVIOR

Unlike many other bird species, hummingbirds do not gather in a group to eat. They don't gather in groups to sleep or **migrate**, either. Hummingbirds are only found together for mating and possibly to share a feeder.

Some hummingbirds are highly territorial. Males **aggressively** defend their territory, which is chosen for its supply of food and water. Many males perch on high, obvious branches. This is both a visual warning to **intruders** and a place to monitor their home.

Hummingbirds will chase after invaders, including other hummingbirds, larger birds, bees, and butterflies. This is often to defend food sources. Females will defend the area around a nest.

With all this fighting and defending, it would seem the hummingbird is a very busy creature. Yet the tiny bird spends more than half of its time perched on a branch, resting. This conserves energy for flying, hovering, and feeding. Hummingbirds also **preen** themselves while perched.

IN AND OUT

A hummingbird takes 250 breaths every minute. Compare that with humans, who generally take just 16 breaths each minute!

Many hummingbirds go into **torpor** at night. But, they do not do this on all nights. Torpor allows the hummingbird's body to preserve energy by dropping its heart rate, slowing its breathing, and dropping its body temperature. It can last 8 to 14 hours. A hummingbird can't fully wake up right away. Its body temperature must rise before it flies again.

Rain, sprinklers, waterfall spray, and streams provide baths for hummingbirds!

COMMUNICATION

Hummingbirds use calls, songs, chirps, buzzing, chatter, and other noises to communicate. Calls vary greatly. They depend on the hummingbird's species and whether it is male or female. Some calls are warnings or an alert to danger. Others distract trespassers. Quiet, begging calls may be from **nestlings** saying, "I'm hungry!"

Some calls are long and melodic. These are often mating calls, but they also warn off predators. The hummingbird's "humming" is not a call. But, scientists believe that even this sound is a form of communication. For example, the dive-bombing male's humming adds to his call for a mate!

Hummingbirds also communicate through visual display. A flashing, closely hovering hummingbird says, "Get lost!" The male's aerial show says "Pick me!" when competing for a mate. He may also show off his **gorget** feathers.

WHAT'S THAT SOUND?
The hummingbird's name comes from the humming sound its feathers make when it is flying.

Hummingbirds pant
to cool off.

ENEMIES & DEFENSES

What do hummingbirds need to scare away? With their speed and **agility**, adult hummingbirds are fairly safe from predators. However, eggs and **nestlings** are easy targets.

Hummingbird predators include larger birds such as owls, falcons, and toucans. Roadrunners, orioles, kestrels, hawks, and bats are also threats. In addition, frogs, fish, dragonflies, spiders, and praying mantises can attack hummingbirds. Snakes like to feast on tiny hummingbirds, too.

Hummingbirds use many defenses to protect themselves. Males flash **intruders** with their bright feathers and make themselves appear larger. Hummingbirds chase and dive-bomb threats. Male and female hummingbirds also fight with their bills and use their claws.

The female hummingbird is protective of her young. She is careful not to draw attention to their nest. She even flies in zigzag and other patterns to avoid leading predators to her young. Plus, she carefully blends her nest into its surroundings.

Eyelash vipers in Costa Rica know rufous-tailed hummingbirds visit certain flowers, so they lie in wait for a tasty meal!

CONSERVATION

The hummingbird faces human-made threats as well. The greatest threat is loss of **habitat**. Exposure to **pesticides** can also harm the hummingbird. The bird's small bill can get stuck in window screens. In addition, humans throughout history have hunted the hummingbird for its colorful feathers and for sport.

Hummingbirds have some ability to adapt to other habitats. However, many species are not successful due to loss of food sources and nesting spots. For these reasons, the **IUCN** lists a number of hummingbird species as vulnerable, **endangered**, critically endangered, or extinct. Luckily, most of the more than 300 hummingbird species are considered least concern.

Many North American hummingbird populations are stable. Feeders and flower beds supply all the necessary food. Small woodlands allow for nesting. In addition, the **Migratory Bird Treaty Act** protects most of these beautiful, entertaining birds. That means hummingbirds are more likely to visit your backyard!

People have long
been fascinated by
the hummingbird's
beautiful feathers.

GLOSSARY

aggressive (uh-GREH-sihv) - displaying hostility.

agility - the ability to move quickly and easily.

endangered - in danger of becoming extinct.

environment - all the surroundings that affect the growth and well-being of a living thing.

evolve - to develop gradually.

fledgling - a young bird that has gained its feathers and can leave the nest.

genera - more than one genus. A genus is a group that scientists use to classify similar plants or animals. It ranks above a species and below a family.

gorget (GAWR-juht) - a specially colored area on the throat.

habitat - a place where a living thing is naturally found.

hemisphere - one half of Earth.

incubate - to keep eggs warm, often by sitting on them, so they will hatch.

intruder - one who enters without being asked or wanted.

iridescent (ihr-uh-DEH-suhnt) - shining with many different colors when viewed from different angles.

IUCN - the International Union for Conservation of Nature. The IUCN is a global environmental organization focused on conservation.

lush - having a lot of growth and green vegetation.

migrate - to move from one place to another, often to find food.

Migratory Bird Treaty Act - a law that protects migratory birds, their eggs, and their nests from hunting, capture, or possession.

nestling - a young bird that cannot yet leave the nest.

New World - the continents of the western half of Earth.

ornithologist (awr-nuh-THAH-luh-juhst) - a scientist who studies birds.

pesticide (PEHS-tuh-side) - a substance used to destroy pests.

pollinate - to carry pollen from one part of a flower or plant to another.

porous - having small holes that allow air or liquids to pass through.

preen - to use the bill to groom feathers.

regurgitate (ree-GUHR-juh-tayt) - to throw back out again, especially partly broken down food.

sea level - the level of the ocean's surface. Land elevations and sea depths are measured from sea level.

torpor - a state of slowed body and mind activity.

tropics - an area extending just north and south of Earth's equator.

ultraviolet - relating to a type of light that cannot be seen with the human eye.

WEBSITES

To learn more about Backyard Animals, visit **booklinks.abdopublishing.com**. These links are routinely monitored and updated to provide the most current information available.

INDEX

A

Apodiformes (order) 4

B

bill 12, 18, 20, 26, 28
bird feeder 9, 18, 22, 28
body 12, 14, 17, 20, 23

C

claws 12, 26
color 12, 14, 16
communication 16, 24

D

defenses 12, 14, 16, 17, 22, 24, 26

E

eggs 16, 17, 26
eyes 12

F

feathers 24, 26, 28
feet 12, 13
food 9, 11, 12, 16, 17, 18, 20, 22, 28

H

habitat 6, 8, 9, 11, 20, 28
head 12, 14
history 6, 28

I

IUCN 28

L

legs 12
life span 17

M

migration 6, 11, 18, 22
Migratory Bird Treaty Act 28

N

nest 14, 16, 17, 22, 26, 28

P

perching 13, 22
Phaethornithinae (subfamily) 4
preening 22

R

range 4, 6, 8, 18, 28
reproduction 16, 22, 24

S

senses 12, 17
size 11, 12, 13, 14, 16, 17, 20
speed 14, 26

T

tail 14
threats 12, 14, 22, 24, 26, 28
toes 12
tongue 18
torpor 23
Trochilidae (family) 4
Trochilinae (subfamily) 4

W

water 20, 22
wings 4, 13, 14

Y

young 11, 14, 17, 20, 24, 26